Victory!

Poems by Jake Frost

1

For My Family

Victory!

Poems by Jake Frost

Table of Contents

Christmas Poems

Victory!

Palm fronds strewn upon the road
Covered the dust where the donkey strode
That carried the King of Peace to war
And well He knew what lay in store

The kiss, the scourge, and the crown
Thrice His falling to the ground
Then His cross lifted high
Between the earth and the sky

All this He knew yet He obeyed
And at last Adam's dragon slayed
The dark of the tomb He would see
But after three days, *victory*!

The Aedicule enclosing the empty tomb of Jesus located
within The Church of the Holy Sepulcher in Jerusalem

Church of St. Peter in Gallicantu

Historical Note on Gallicantu

Gallicantu, Latin for "Cock's Crow," is the name of *The Church of Saint Peter in Gallicantu* located where the High Priest Caiaphas once had his palace. It was here that Jesus was taken after being seized in the Garden of Gethsemane. Saint Peter followed the High Priest's soldiers as they brought Jesus and entered the palace grounds after them to see what would happen. It was here that Christ's prophecy was fulfilled when Saint Peter three times denied Christ before the cock crowed. After Saint Peter's third denial the cock immediately crowed and then Jesus turned and looked at Saint Peter. Saint Peter broke down and fled weeping.

Atop the Church of St. Peter in Gallicantu

9

The Garden of Gethsemane

In The Garden

Jesus walked out into the night
Going from the Upper Room
Toward the Mount of Olives' height
Through the shadowed starlit gloom

He walked through the Kidron Valley
To a place He often went
The Garden of Gethsemane
With its air of fragrant scent

Here Jesus liked to come to pray
And this night He needed prayer
For now before Him lay the way
Of the cross that He would bear

He was sorrowful unto death
As before Him He saw loom
The rattle of His dying breath
Then the darkness of the tomb

He asked that His disciples keep
Watch with Him as came the hour
When sinful men His life to reap
Would have Him in their power

Further aside with Him He drew
To pray against temptation
Peter, James, and John, the three who
Saw The Transfiguration

Then by Himself He went apart
Another stone's throw away
In the agony of His heart
He kneeled on the earth to pray

The earth that Adam's curse had sown
To yield thistle and the thorn
The day death came to flesh and bone
And Creation's rift was torn

When knowing well what was God's will
Adam chose to disobey
Letting the serpent's fell lies fill
And then turn his heart away

Adam chose his own will to reign
Alone supreme over all
And God, Who gave him life, disdain
So he brought on man The Fall

Naked once grace was cast aside
Adam sought for shadows deep
Where in The Garden he might hide
In Eden, God bade him keep

Where in evenings he had heard
As God walked amid the shade
Spoken by God the Living Word
Through which all that is was made

Now this night this same earth would know
The blood of His agony
That fallen from Our Lord would sow
The ground of Gethsemane

As in Eden, with sword aflame,
God sent His angel to stand,
So too an angel of God now came
To strengthen The Son of Man

Then for a moment came a hush
As Creation paused to wait
To hear within The Garden lush
Words to change its fallen fate

When in ancient Gethsemane
To the Father prayed the Son,
"Please let his chalice pass from Me,"
"But Your will, not Mine, be done."

Jesus arose from where He prayed
He knew the hour was at hand
The ancient debt would now be paid
For all by The Son of Man

Peter, James, and John were asleep
He asked, "Do you take your rest?"
"Could you not even one hour keep,"
"Watch with me before the test?"

"Willing though the spirit may be,"
"Even still the flesh is weak."
"Enough, the hour comes on Me,"
"See the traitor as I speak."

To The Garden there entered in
To achieve his wicked end,
The betrayal to men of sin
Of the One he called his friend,

Judas, who by his lips would slay
And Jesus asked, "What is this?"
"Truly, tell Me, would you betray,"
"The Son of Man with a kiss?"

With the betrayer was a crowd
Which had come out stealthily
After descended night's dark shroud
To wrap them in secrecy

"Why come in dark when none can see?"
Jesus asked in the torch's sheen
Their reply was to ask if He
Were Jesus the Nazarene?

Then in answer He said, "I AM."
And sudden as a jar broken
Each felt the Word into him slam
The Son of Man had spoken

Like a thunderclap fell the blow
They tumbled and none could stand
Before the Word were all laid low
Breathed out by The Son of Man

"If it is Me you seek," said He,
"Leave the other ones alone."
So in accord with prophecy
None would be lost of His own

Then to seize Jesus in their grasp
The temple guards rushed near
His own sword then did Peter clasp
And struck from a slave his ear

Jesus spoke, knowing what must be,
"No More! Put your sword away!"
"The Father gave this cup to Me,"
"And His Will I shall obey."

Then to the man in bondage came
Our Savior's healing power
John said that Malchus was his name
Who Our Lord restored that hour

The name Malchus has a meaning,
A king does it signify,
Like the three of angel-dreaming
Who saw The Star in the sky

In the beginning man was king
In The Garden ruling all
Before the chains that sin would bring
Enslaved him at The Fall

And that night the slave-king Malchus
In The Garden met the Lord
Who healed his wounded mortal dust
And would break the bondman's chord

Swords and clubs in their hands they bore
Jesus asked, "Am I a thief?"
"That you come out arrayed for war?"
"With your sword drawn from its sheath?"

"Each day in the temple I taught,"
"While daylight shimmered around,"
"If any day you would have sought,"
"Me that day you would have found."

His disciples all were scattered
What was next to come none knew
How by His gaze would be shattered
The Rock at *Gallicantu*

In nakedness again was man
Having shed the garment of grace
As again into The Garden he ran
To seek a hiding place

The sinners seized and bound the Lord
As all His disciples fled
Then by those armed with club and sword
From The Garden He was led

But there the story does not end
In The Garden it begins
The Temple veil is yet to rend
When Jesus dies for our sins

Then Magdalen comes to the tomb
After the days numbered three
To what she thinks a place of doom
There The Gardener to see

When Abraham Looked

I wander at night far
When the moon is high
Out under the bright stars
And gaze at the sky

God told Abraham see
The stars in the sky
Your descendants shall be
As the stars on high

When Abraham looked at
The stars did he see
One star in the night that
Shown that night for me

All God's children one day
Shall shine like the sun
Let me shine God, I pray,
When that day has come

Flaming Arrows

The Five Hundred Nations in the days of old
Wrote in fire crimson-gold

In the heavens with feathered shafts set alight
In the dark burning bright

From the bent bow sent aflame into the sky
From the string springing high

When the setting sun fell below the world's rim
And skies grew dark and dim

Then swifter than galloping horses there rode
Through the night the fire code

For all who knew what it was they looked upon
In the dark before the dawn

And like flaming arrows the stars bear at night
A message with their light

For there where need nothing ever be they shine
Made by a Hand Divine

That hung them there and told Abraham to see
And know what Man can be

Historical Note on *Flaming Arrows*

The Five Hundred Nations were the 500 different nations of North American Indians. They used flaming arrows shot into the sky at night to communicate via code.

Ruins of Mount Grace Priory, England,
destroyed by Henry VIII in 1539

Sun Silvered Windows

In the sun silvered windows
The shining sunset glows

With the bright day's final spark
Before there falls the dark

Tall windows in walls of stone
That sun and moon have known

With the passing of the years
Through this vale of tears

In our fathers' fathers' days
Were these windows glazed

And placed within these walls of stone
Where bright the sunlight shown

Upon the church that they made
Where our parents prayed

That in the gathering night
Still might shine the light

Hl. Franziska.
Ste Françoise.

1860 prayer card from Germany of
Saint Frances of Rome

Historical Note on Saint Frances of Rome

Saint Frances of Rome was born in 1384 and died in 1440. She was a wife and mother who worked raising her children and making a home for her family. She understood the important sanctity of the home and said that those entrusted with a family must sometimes leave God at the altar and find Him in their service to their families in their own home.

She had many spiritual gifts, including visions of her guardian angel. Once when she was home attempting to spend quiet time in prayer she was repeatedly interrupted as she tried to read a prayer book. At each interruption, she patiently set aside the prayer book and went to attend to the need at hand. After the last such interruption she discovered the lettering of her prayer book had been miraculously gilt in gold.

The Prayer of Saint Frances of Rome

Mine is the prayer of Saint Frances of Rome
Who raised her children and made a home
It's not prayed straight through from the start
For interruptions lie at its heart

That come from little hands that tug
And little souls that need a hug

It's a prayer that welcomes another's need
That pauses to water the tiny seed

That stoops to help another grow
And delights to let another know

That they are loved and held dear
It's a prayer of giving with good cheer

It's prayed in time and prayed in care
In knots gently brushed from tangled hair

In sacrifice and small deeds done
Constantly as the hours run

Through the day and through the night
Giving each moment a widow's mite

26

Of all I am and do and say
And in the giving with love I pray

A humble prayer no one else can see
Except Jesus who keeps me company

Saint Frances of Rome

Historical Note on Oceanus

Oceanus Hopkins was born aboard the Mayflower during the Pilgrims' Atlantic crossing in 1620. He died in the New World sometime after the Pilgrims landed at Plymouth Rock and before 1627, the exact dates of his birth and death, like his gravesite, being unknown.

Portico over Plymouth Rock, Plymouth, Massachusetts

Oceanus

Oceanus was born upon the waves
Between the Old World and the New
With spar and mast set in the sign that saves
Above where the tempest blew

He was born to journey upon the barque
Bound from birth for the Unknown Shore
His cradle a Pilgrims' pitching ark
His lullaby an ocean's roar

Cleaving heaving seas to the Unknown Shore
Flying before the wild winds that roam
To that bright New Land never seen before
Where beyond all sea and storm lay home

The Mayflower at Sea

An American Dream

Every time a dream first begins
In every underdog who fights and wins

In every second chance to try
To shine like Abraham's stars in the sky

In every heart that's free and brave
It shines like a light through the storm to save

And through the darkness it's shining still
Like the Shining City upon the hill

Give thanks to God Who came to redeem
For giving us an American Dream

Washington Crossing the Delaware

The Baptistry of Saint John in Pisa, Italy

Reborn in Water

Rain shakes down from the crabapple trees
From purple petals stirred in the breeze
Rain drums softly falling on the earth
The soft, cool rain of Spring's rebirth

Reborn in water the world's renewed
As when Moses through the waves once hewed
Or after the days of dark that numbered three
Paul was baptized and could finally see

So go with Joshua across the Jordan dry
Where once like thunder came from the sky
The Father's own voice when John was done
Saying: "This is my beloved Son."

Set sail with Noah upon the ark
Hear Jesus speak from Saint Peter's barque
Go wash in Siloam's pool and be
After the darkness at last set free

The Poet's Path

I've picked up some tricks along the way
Some turns of the tongue and things to say

But the surest guide that I've found
Is to hear your lines and how they sound

Don't fuss too much about the rules
Of iambic pentameter taught in schools

The heart of poetry's rhythm and rhyme
Is eternal truth spoken in time

The Poet's Corner, Westminster Abbey, London

The Old Church Upon the Hill

To the old church upon the hill
    I shall go to sit awhile and be still

To be for a time there alone
And watch the sunlight wash upon the stone

And mark the sky's swift changing moods
Displayed on the pile over which it broods

Watching as light and shadow play
In patterns as the moments pass away

And take some time to contemplate
The truth, and choose, before it is too late

St. Mary's Chapel at the Saint Paul Seminary, St Paul, MN,
the seminary attended by Servant of God Fulton J. Sheen

The Frost Family Journal

My Great-Great-Grandfather David Henry Frost began a family journal on Thanksgiving Day, November 28, 1878, in Belle Plaine, Iowa, as the family was preparing to move farther west to Nebraska. He included with his first entry a clipping of the magazine piece which inspired him to begin The Frost Family Journal:

> In a certain farm house twenty years ago, a great plank book was kept and labeled Home Journal. Every night somebody made an entry into it. Father set down the sale of the calves or mother the cut of baby's eye tooth; or perhaps Jenny wrote a full account of the sleighing party last night, or Bob the proceedings of the Phi Beta club; or Tom scrawled, "Tried my new gun. Bully."
>
> ***
>
> . . . nothing could have served better to bind that family of head-strong boys and girls together than keeping of this book. They come back to the old homestead now—men and women with grizzled hair, to see their mother still living, and turn over its pages reverently with many a hearty laugh, or the tears coming to their eyes. It is their childhood come back again in visionable shape.

From the first entry made in the Frost Family Journal four generations ago, journals were kept for another 43 years. They comprise a real treasure, recording moments such as the time in 1878 when my Great-Great-Aunt at the family farm out on the prairie danced a whole in the *roof*:

> Thea got up an entirely novel entertainment . . . Climbing upon the rude shanty which serves as a stable for Ellery's pony, she began dancing a lively jig on the roof. The boards proved unequal to this experience and she broke through, falling down into the stable by the side of the pony. Both she and the pony were very much frightened.

Fortunately neither aunt nor equine were injured.

When not dancing on the roof, among other pursuits my ancestors wrote poetry. "The Meadow Lark" was written by Elizabeth Marion Frost, another of my Great-Great-Aunts and a sister of Thea the Rooftop-High-Stepper. The poem appears in her journal under the date of March 15, 1887, 9 years after the first entry was made in the original Family Journal, and after the family had resettled in Nebraska. Marion, as she was called by her family, was a great poet, though as far as I can determine she never published anything in her lifetime. I am honored to now present this poem of hers over a century after she first penned these lines.

The Meadow Lark

A True Story of the Day

By Elizabeth Marion Frost

Dated March 15, 1887

Oh, wild the east wind bloweth
And slow the winter goeth;
The sky is cold and gray,
And weary seems the day.

But listen, listen, hear!
What voice is that so near?
The meadow lark is singing!
Tiding of spring-time bringing!

God's blessings on the bird
That bringeth us that word,
Our hearts fly upward in his song,
Borne by its sweetness, pure and strong.

Within a lowly cabin, I,
Weary, upon a sick bed lie;
And listen to the restless feet
Upon the roof—a trampling sweet.

He sings! The clouds have rolled away;
It seems a happy summer day;
The sun shines bright, the air is blessed,
And all is peace and joy and rest.

He sings! The merry brook I hear
That charmed my childhood's listening ear;
My bare feet in the stream I lave,
And watch each twisted, rippling wave.

He sings again, and now it seems
(His song is mingled with my dreams.)
That he a lily fair must be,
Growing upon a sunny lea.

A slender stalk the flower upraises;
The whispering wind its beauty praises;
Softly and low the lily sings;
Deep in my heart its music rings.

This is the song the meadow lark sings
When he rests his happy wings;
And his song doth banish sadness,
Leaveth room for naught but gladness.

Drawn in Chalk

Drawn in chalk
On my sidewalk
A smiling face I see

It was made
As children played
And brings a smile to me

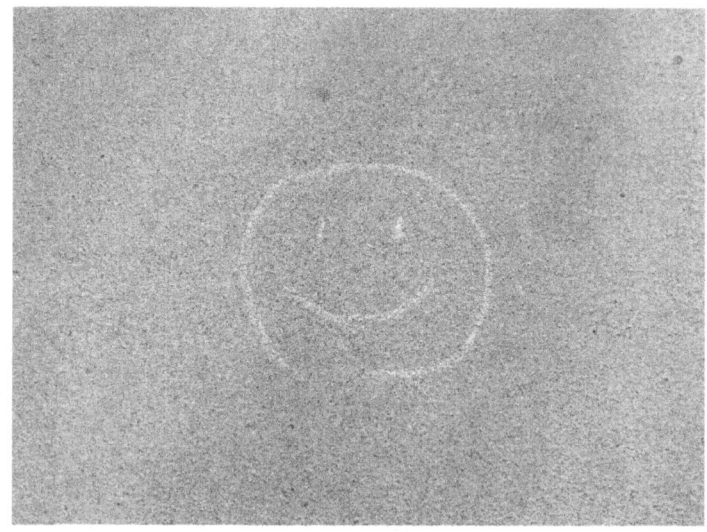

Little Graces

Little graces
In little faces
Everywhere abound

Where children live
The love God gives
Every day is found

A Parent's Prayer

In bits and parts
And fits and starts
I pray all through the day

In things I do
With love for you
As I give myself away

The Question

If the years gone-by were given me
To live over once again
I would live them so that I could see
What it was I might have been

I would tell the truth and dare and try
I'd believe in bigger dreams
More than worry *how* I'd ponder *why*
And enjoy the little things

I'd believe in *me* and do my best
Let the chips fall where they may
I'd work hard and then I'd take my rest
And be thankful for each day

But though all those years have flown away
Still a question stays for me
One that I must answer now today
Of who yet I still might be

As Memories Walk With Me

The wind in the trees like old memories
Murmurs around me tonight
As ragged clouds fly through the moonlit sky
Sailing on silvery light

A thrill and a rush in the still and hush
When the wind roars in the tree
Fills all the night in the silvery light
As memories walk with me

Historical Note on Saint Martin's Day

World War I ended on Armistice Day, also called Remembrance Day, on the 11th hour of the 11th day of the 11th month of 1918, which day (November 11) is also the Feast Day of Saint Martin of Tours.

Saint Martin was named for Mars, the god of war, and became a soldier in the Roman army. Then later Saint Martin laid down his arms in exchange for the peace of Christ, leaving the legions and taking up religious life, making his feast day symbolic for peace treaties.

Saint Martin was born in 316 AD in Hungary where he enlisted in the Roman army. He was stationed in France and spent most of the rest of his life there. While riding one cold winter evening he met a poor man at the gates of Amiens who was begging, naked and cold, outside the city walls. Saint Martin cut his heavy military cloak in two with his sword and gave half of it to the beggar. That night Jesus came to Saint Martin in a dream and revealed to Saint Martin that it had been He, Jesus Himself, who had been the poor beggar Martin clothed with half of his military cloak.

Saint Martin was baptized and left the legions, eventually becoming Bishop of Tours.

The remaining half of Saint Martin's cloak became a treasured relic of the kings of France who carried it with them into battle. As the French armies marched the Capella, which is Latin for "little cape" (little since the cloak was half its former size thanks to Saint Martin's impromptu sword-stroke tailoring), was kept in a small tent of its own that accompanied the army. Capella came to refer to the tent as well as the cloak and eventually evolved into the word "chapel."

Saint Martin died in 397 AD and was buried at Tours. Over the centuries his tomb became a center of pilgrimage and a great cathedral was built on the site. However, the cathedral was sacked by Vikings in 996 and then by Protestants in 1562, who also destroyed most of Saint Martin's relics. Finally, what remained of Saint Martin's tomb and cathedral were demolished by the militant atheists of the French revolution in 1793. Almost a hundred years later, Saint Martin's tomb was re-discovered and a new Basilica of Saint Martin was built in 1886.

Tomb of Saint Martin in the Cathedral of Saint Martin in Tours, France

World War I Flanders Field American Cemetery and Memorial in Waregem, Belgium

In November We Remember

In November we remember
Those who have left for the farther shore
As the ringing rolls from the bell that tolls
For the ones who went before

Through the mist and cold that enfold
A land fallow with autumn's rest
Clanging carries and lingering, tarries
Like their memories, forever blessed

Memories that wake the longing ache
For those we still love dear
Until the sunset sky is baptized by
The course of a silent tear

A silent tear as we persevere
On our way to that distant shore
There to meet and embracing greet
The ones who went before

Autumn's Ember

Autumn's ember is November
When the fires of Fall still glow
In the colors of leaves on rain black trees
That shake in the winds that blow

Oranges and reds like sunset spreads
Blazing across the skies
And deeper hues from purpled views
At dusk when the deer arise

Each leaf and shade an offering made
Through the seasons as they spin
The thread of life, through joy and strife,
God's gift of love to men

Christmas Poems

A Christmas Prayer

I lie on the couch by the Christmas tree
With an old, soft blanket covering me

The fire on the grate is burning low
Casting a ruddy, golden glow

Outside I hear the winds that sigh
And swirl the snows through the sky

The children all are tucked in bed
Matthew and Luke have both been read

As off to sleep I drift away
One final, small prayer I say:

"Thank you, Lord, for Christmas Day."

Winter Dreams

We were tucked in our blankets in bed
Drowsy with sleep drawing near
When in tiptoed our Dad and said,
"It's the first snow of the year!"

To the living room we rushed
Where curtains were open wide
And by beauty there were hushed
As we gazed on the wonder outside

Everywhere snowflakes flew
In the golden streetlamp's glow
On billowing gusts that blew
There shimmered the swirl of snow

In a world of mystery
Where sang angels in the night
And Kings of Epiphany
Followed the Star shining bright

Though for long we watched the storm
We returned to bed, it seems
For in blankets soft and warm
We drifted in winter dreams

A Christmas Eve Prayer

When the snows of winter
Lie deep upon the hill
And the Christmas candle
Burns on the windowsill

And the tree is decorated
With ornaments and lights
And all the world is waiting
For the joy that comes tonight

Christmas angels gather
And all the heavens fill
With their song of peace
To all men of good will

For the world tonight
I make a Christmas prayer
That the love of Jesus
Come to all men everywhere

A Child Born in the Cold

In the dark of the first Christmas
While angels sang their hymns of old
A mother gave her kiss
To a Child born in the cold

In the dark of the first Christmas
While kings brought frankincense, myrrh, and gold
A father gave his kiss
To a Child born in the cold

Think of what God gave
There is nothing He'll withhold
He gave to us His Son
A Child born in the cold

Gloria In Excelsis Deo Chapel in Angels' Field near Bethlehem where angels appeared to shepherds in the fields at night

Ice and Ember Still Remember

Winter's white illumines night
With moonshine on the snow
While red sparks rise to starry skies
From the crackling fire's glow

The sparks shine bright against the night
Amid the falling snow
That swirling drifts and falls and lifts
On the howling winds that blow

Ice and ember still remember
A long-ago night like this
When turning from a fire burning
Against the cold of winter's kiss

Men raised their eyes to the skies
And a weary world and worn
Heard the cry from angels high
"Christ your King is born!"

When the Wind Whips Round Me Cold

When the wind whips round me cold
Whispers from the days of old
Mingle in its moan and whine
Tales of winter's sacred time

When appeared in battle helm
Angels come from heaven's realm
Marching through the skies at night
While shepherds gazed at the sight

From on high the angels said:
"Go now to His manger-bed,"
"You will find Him swaddled there,"
"In the Blessed Lady's care."

"Daniel's count of years is done,"
"Unto you is born the Son,"
"The kingdom now is at hand,"
"Of the Christ, The Son of Man."

"To all good men everywhere,"
"Comes now Royal David's heir,"
"Jacob's star is shining bright,"
"Your Savior has come this night."

And still upon the wintry blast
There echoes yet from the past
The angel's call from that night
When in the dark there came The Light:

"Rejoice! Rejoice! All the earth!"
"Your King has come at His birth!"

The Three Kings

Caspar, Melchior, and Balthasar
The kings who followed the angel-star
From different places upon the earth
Were led by prophecies to His birth

One from Africa of Sheba's gold
One from Asia of the silken fold
One from Europe of the Occident
Each one to far Bethlehem was sent

They came to represent every land
And in their years every age of man
One young, one prime, and one old
Borne on dromedaries through the cold

Riding across shifting sands that sigh
As unseen winds whisper through the sky
Through the nights when heaven's grandeur lay
A-shimmer across the Milky Way

The Three Kings, Nativity of Our Lord Church, St. Paul, Minnesota

Each left the country of his own home
Each left an ancestral throne to roam
In quest of a prophecy fulfilled
As for these three kings it had been willed

Earthly riches they considered naught
When compared to what it was they sought
For worth more to man than all the earth
Was the gift that was given at His birth

Bright gold they brought for the King of kings
Who with power peace and justice brings
And myrrh which a prophet signifies
Also means true flesh of man who dies

And frankincense, as did Aaron's rod,
Showed that the Child was a priest of God
Yet still frankincense means something more
For its incense opens heaven's door

Made of fragrant resin from the tree
It represents divinity
For at Bethlehem was born in straw
The coming God-Man Isaiah saw

As Daniel, who read upon the wall
For King Belshazzar the angel's scrawl,
Said the stone cut by no human hand
Would come that day as The Son of Man

So was the worship the three kings gave
To Our Lady's Baby born to save
Not that due to any earthly throne
But worship reserved to God alone

And as angels spoke to these three kings
In their dreams revealing hidden things
So it was when came their time to leave
They knew what webs Herod sought to weave

And the angel's word they did obey
And left for home by another way
Waiting for when Thomas would baptize
They who had seen God's face with their own eyes

Now in the Cathedral of Cologne
In a reliquary rest the bones
Of Caspar, Melchior, and Balthasar
The kings who followed the angel-star

Who look waiting for the day to come
When in glory shall return The Son
And they shall arise to see once more
The face that once they beheld before

Reliquary holding the earthly remains of The Three Kings, Saint Caspar, Saint Melchior, and Saint Balthasar, in Cologne Cathedral, Cologne, Germany

Explanatory Note on the Baptism by Thomas

Saint Thomas the Apostle, also known as "Doubting Thomas," is said to have baptized Saints Caspar, Melchior, and Balthasar somewhere in the East after the resurrection of Jesus.

Image Credits

Cover, the Church of the Holy Sepulcher, from
www.commons.wikimedia.org; URL:
https://commons.wikimedia.org/wiki/File:Holy_Selupcre_2
.JPG; Author: ReeveJ; Description/Title: Church of the Holy
Sepulchre; License: Creative Commons Attribution-Share
Alike 3.0 Unreported; Date: 15 August 2014

Page 6, illustration of Jesus entering Jerusalem on Palm
Sunday; from www.commons.wikimedia.org; URL:
https://commons.wikimedia.org/wiki/File:Jesus_entry_into
_Jerusalem.jpg ; Author: Julius Schnorr von Carolsfeld;
license: Public Domain; date: 1860

Page 7, Aedicule containing the empty tomb of Jesus, from
www.commons.wikimedia.org, URL:
https://commons.wikimedia.org/wiki/File:Aedicule_which_
supposedly_encloses_the_tomb_of_Jesus-LR1.jpg; Author:
Jlascar; Description/Title: The Church of the Holy
Sepulchre is a church within the Christian Quarter of the
walled Old City of Jerusalem. It is a few steps away from
the Muristan. The site is venerated as Calvary (Golgatha),
where Jesus was crucified, and is said to also contain the
place where Jesus was buried; License: Creative Commons
Attribution 2.0 Generic; Date: 4 September 2012

Page 8, The Church of Saint Peter in Gallicantu, from
www.commons.wikimedia.org; URL:
https://commons.wikimedia.org/wiki/File:Jerusalem_St._P
eter_in_Gallicantu_1.JPG; Author: Zairon;
Description/Title: St. Peter in Gallicantu, Jerusalem, Israel;

License: Creative Commons Attriubtion-Share Alike 4.0 International; Date: 5 March 214

Page 9, Atop the Church of St. Peter in Gallicantu; from: www.commons.wikimedia.org; URL: https://commons.wikimedia.org/wiki/File:Saint_Peter_in_Gallicantu_(9198076449).jpg; Author: someone10x; Description/Title: Saint Peter in Gallicantu; License: Creative Commons Attribution 2.0 Generic; Date: 7 October 2009

Page 10, the Garden of Gethsemane, from www.commons.wikimedia.org, URL: https://commons.wikimedia.org/wiki/File:%D0%9EId_Olive_trees_in_the_Garden_of_Gethsemane,_07.jpg; Author: Beko; Description/Title: Very old olive trees in the Garden of Gethsemane, where according to the Bible Jesus was praying before crucifixion; License: Creative Commons Attribution-Share Alike 4.0 International; Date: 7 November 2018;

Page 19, 1860 Bible Illustration; from www.commons.wikimedia.org; URL: https://commons.wikimedia.org/wiki/File:Schnorr_von_Carolsfeld_Bibel_in_Bildern_1860_004.png; Author: Julius Schnorr von Carolsfeld; License: Public Domain; Date: 1860

Page 21, line drawing of an arrowhead; from www.commons.wikimedia.org; URL: https://commons.wikimedia.org/wiki/File:PSM_V02_D362_Arrow_head.jpg; Author: unknown; License: Public Domain, Date: 1872 or 1873

Page 21, line drawing of an arrow; from
www.commons.wikimedia.org; URL:
https://commons.wikimedia.org/wiki/File:Arrow_(PSF).png
Author: Pearson Scott Foresman; License: Public Domain;
Date: 2008

Page 22, ruins of Mount Grace Priory; from:
www.commons.wikimedia.org; URL:
https://commons.wikimedia.org/wiki/File:Sunlight_pours_t
hrough_arched_windows_-_geograph.org.uk_-
_1054548.jpg; Author: Carol Rose; Description/Title:
Sunlight pours through arched windows The 'windows' are
actually reflected light and shade onto the old wall next to
the doorway; License: Creative Commons Attribution-
Share Alike 2.0 Generic; Date: 15 November 2008

Page 24, prayer card of Saint Frances of Rome; from:
www.commons.wikimedia.org; URL:
https://commons.wikimedia.org/wiki/File:Frances_of_Rom
e.jpg; Author: unknown; Description/Title:
Andachtsbildchen hl. Franziska, Chromolithographie, 1861,
8 x 12 cm; License: Public Domain; Date: 1861

Page 27, statue of Saint Frances of Rome; from:
www.commons.wikimedia.org; URL:
https://commons.wikimedia.org/wiki/File:Qu%C3%A9m%C
3%A9n%C3%A9ven_(29)_Chapelle_Notre-
Dame_de_Kergoat_Statue_11.JPG; Author: GO69;
Description/Title: Chapelle Notre-Dame de Kergoat en
Quéménéven (29). Statue de Sainte-Françoise; License:
Creative Commons Attribution-Share Alike 4.0
International; Date: 21 April 2012

Page 28, Plymouth Rock Portico; from:
www.commons.wikimedia.org; URL:
https://commons.wikimedia.org/wiki/File:Plymouth_Rock,
_Water_St,_Plymouth_(493637)_(11108906366).jpg;
Author: Robert Linsdall from St. Andrew's, Canada;
Description/Title: Plymouth Rock, Water St, Plymouth,
Massachusetts, United States; License: Creative Commons
Attribution 2.0 Generic; 2 October 2013

Page 29, The Mayflower at Sea; from:
www.commons.wikimedia.org; URL:
https://commons.wikimedia.org/wiki/File:The_Mayflower_
at_sea.jpg; Author: John Clark Ridpath; Description/Title:
The Mayflower at Sea; License: Public Domain; Date: 1893

Page 30, Washington Crossing the Delaware; from:
www.commons.wikimedia.org; URL:
https://commons.wikimedia.org/wiki/File:Washington_Cro
ssing_the_Delaware_by_Emanuel_Leutze,_MMA-
NYC,_1851.jpg; Author: Emanuel Leutze;
Description/Title: Washington Crossing the Delaware;
License: Public Domain; Date: 1851

Page 31, God showing Abraham the stars of the sky; from:
www.commons.wikimedia.org; URL:
https://commons.wikimedia.org/wiki/File:Schnorr_von_Ca
rolsfeld_Bibel_in_Bildern_1860_024.png; Author: Julius
Schnorr von Carolsfeld; License: Public Domain; Date:
1860

Page 32, The Baptistry of St. John in Pisa, Italy; from:
www.commons.wikimedia.org; URL:
https://commons.wikimedia.org/wiki/File:Baptistry_(Pisa).j
pg;

Author: Satdeep Gill; Description/Title: Pisa Baptistry in Pisa; License: Creative Commons Attribution-Share Alike 4.0 International; Date: 1 June 2016

Page 34, The Poet's Corner, Westminster Abbey; from: www.commons.wikimedia.org; URL: https://commons.wikimedia.org/wiki/File:Poets_corner.jpg Author: Unknown; License: Public Domain

Page 35, St. Mary's Chapel in Saint Paul, Minnesota, image by Jake Frost

Page 39, Meadow Lark; from: www.commons.wikimedia.org; URL: https://commons.wikimedia.org/wiki/File:Meadow_Lark_(PSF).png; Author: Pearson Scott Foresman; License: Public Domain

Page 40, chalk smiley face, image by Jake Frost

Page 43, trees in the moonlight; from: www.commons.wikimedia.org; URL: https://commons.wikimedia.org/wiki/File:MECHELIN(1894)_p409_Munsterhjelm_-_Forest_Tarn_by_Moonlight.jpg; License: Public Domain; Date: 1894

Page 45, Tomb of Saint Martin of Tours; from: www.commons.wikimedia.org; URL: https://commons.wikimedia.org/wiki/File:Tombeau_de_Saint-Martin_de_Tours.jpg; Author: Tipoune; Description/Title: Tomb of Saint Martin of Tours in the crypt of the basilica; License: Public Domain; Date: 20 December 2008

Page 46, World War I Flanders Field American Cemetery and Memorial; from: www.commons.wikimedia.org; URL: https://commons.wikimedia.org/wiki/File:Flanders_Field_A merican_Cemetery_and_Memorial.jpg; License: Public Domain; Date: May 2007

Page 49, Christmas Candle; from: www.commons.wikimedia.org; URL: https://commons.wikimedia.org/wiki/File:Christmas_Candl e_with_Swag.png; License: Public Domain; Date: 1919

Page 50, Christmas Tree; from: www.commons.wikimedia.org; URL: https://commons.wikimedia.org/wiki/File:Upominek_z_pra c_Stanis%C5%82awa_Jachowicza_68.jpg; License: Public Domain; Date: 1902

Page 52, angel with Christmas tree; from: www.commons.wikimedia.org; URL: https://commons.wikimedia.org/wiki/File:Skizoj11.png; Author: Franz Ullrich; License: Public Domain; Date: 1934

Page 53, illustration of the Nativity, from: www.commons.wikimedia.org; URL: https://commons.wikimedia.org/wiki/File:Vintage_Christm as_illustration_digitally_enhanced_by_rawpixel-com-36.jpg; Author: Rawpixel; Description/Title: De geboorte van Christus by Cornelis Bloemaert (II), after Abraham Bloemaer (1625); License: Creative Commons Attriubtion-Share Alike 4.0 International; Date: 11 October 217

Page 54, In Excelsis Deo Chapel in Angels' Field; from: www.commons.wikimedia.org; URL: https://en.wikipedia.org/wiki/Chapel_of_the_Shepherd's_Field#/media/File:%22Gloria_in_Excelsis_Deo%22_Chapel.JPG; Author: Maskacjusz; License: Creative Commons Attribution-Share Alike 4.0 International; Date: 4 May 2016

Page 57, Angel Army; from: www.commons.wikimedia.org; URL: https://commons.wikimedia.org/wiki/File:Angels%27_army_by_Guariento.jpg; Author: Guariento de Arpo; Description/Title: Angels' Army; License: Public Domain; Date: 1360

Page 58, adoration of the magi; from: www.commons.wikimedia.org; URL: https://commons.wikimedia.org/wiki/File:Schnorr_von_Carolsfeld_Bibel_in_Bildern_1860_169.png; Author: Julius Schnorr von Carolsfeld; License: Public Domain; Date: 1860

Page 59, the three kings following the star; from: www.commons.wikimedia.org; URL: https://commons.wikimedia.org/wiki/File:Illustrations_from_Alden%27s_Prince_of_Peace_c._1890_0013.jpg; License: Public Domain; Date: 1890

Page 60, The Three Kings, Nativity of Our Lord Church, St. Paul, Minnesota, image by Jake Frost

About the Author

Jake Frost has written four previous books:

Catholic Dad, (Mostly) Funny Stories of Faith, Family, and Fatherhood

Catholic Dad 2, More (Mostly) Funny Stories of Faith, Family, and Fatherhood

The Happy Jar—a children's book which he also illustrated, and

From Dust To Stars, Poems by Jake Frost

He is a lawyer and is married with four children.

Made in the USA
Monee, IL
30 June 2020